Journey of Hope
The Games are Over

By Peter Cole

Published by New Generation Publishing in 2013

Copyright © Peter Cole 2013

First Edition

The author asserts the moral right under the Copyright, Designs and Patents Act 1988 to be identified as the author of this work.

All Rights reserved. No part of this publication may be reproduced, stored in a retrieval system or transmitted, in any form or by any means without the prior consent of the author, nor be otherwise circulated in any form of binding or cover other than that which it is published and without a similar condition being imposed on the subsequent purchaser.

www.newgeneration-publishing.com

 **New Generation Publishing**

Contents

Introduction
Dedication
Foreword
Chapter 1: Why do we have Enemies?
Chapter 2: Jealousy and Envy
Chapter 3: Power – It's Positive and negative Aspects
Chapter 4: God, Present Everywhere
Chapter 5: Kindness for Weakness
Chapter 6: Parental Influence
Chapter 7: We all have Choices
Chapter 8: Relationships
Chapter 9: Love Conquers All
Chapter 10: God heal my Pain
Chapter 11: Summarises

INTRODUCTION

To my reader, the problem for all God fearing people to solve is how far they can actively engage in business social work, use the economic and political agencies necessary for doing that work and throw whatever influence they command on the side of social progress. However, taking a tentative position does not meet the evils of present-day social life. Through better laws, better homes and better distribution of work, it is hoped that we shall make better humans. Trouble in life comes slowly, but we can pray against it. The Bible iterates, 'Call upon me in the day of trouble and I will delivery you and you shall glorify my name'.

Great differences of opinion respectfully pertain to this vital and urgent question, but, as time passes and the claims of the poor cry for attention, an increasing light is cast upon the question, and duty becomes plainer. Often, have I tortured my mind to find an answer to these questions in vain. I genuinely believed that if we could educate each person with good principles to make them better at work and at home, then, in a comparatively short time, we should have done all that is necessary for the betterment of society.

There are still those who claim that for a spiritual life, isolation from economic and political issues is necessary, as if these were not also the outcome of the operations of spiritual and ethical principles. Care must be taken to give the individual his rightful place. The regeneration of society cannot supersede the individual's readiness for what is to come.

As individuals we must each play our part in society, without involving ourselves to any human institutions that may render disastrous results to others or ourselves. In the view of what has been written in these pages, we need to allow each other space for growth. Nothing beneficial or abiding that comes is affected by mere physical force. There is neither hope nor outlook for society if Christian ethics be withheld.

DEDICATION

First, thanks to my family for having the patience with me for taking yet another challenge that decreased the amount of time I could spend with them, especially Paullette Aboyade-Cole, my wife, who has made a big sacrifice.

To our children Kaysha, Jonathan and Richard, I must say your growth provides your Mum and me with a constant source of joy and pride.

Thanks to Catherina Dunphy and the Wordsworth reading group for encouragement, emotional support and good advice, without which this book will not have been possible.

I must say to my wife Paullette, it's an honour to share my life, love and business with you.

'A virtuous woman is a crown to her husband: but she that maketh ashamed is as rottenness in his bones' (Proverbs 12:4).

To you all, I owe a depth of gratitude for your ceaseless and untiring efforts.

FOREWORD

In the following pages, I have examined *'My Journey of Hope—The Games Are Over'*. It is only possible, I submit, to fully appreciate its content and value its far-reaching implications when the steps and stages in the universal quest for moral values are carefully traced. I have attempted to rapidly traverse the wide field of ethical history, and, over the past few years, I've found that I finally have the time and life experiences needed to write about something that is at least semi-meaningful.

The review will, I trust, justify the reasoned claim that I have offered in favour of the supreme value of a colourful life, one driven by a desire to achieve, to support my family and those around me and, importantly for me, to follow a good, Christian life. I have adduced evidence to prove that Christian ethics are directly related to the Person of Christ, which makes me adopt these higher spiritual teachings and recognise the great spiritual and moral transformation of the lives of men that He came to affect.

The path of life I've followed has not always been smooth or well supported. But our Lord gave to me a moral life, new motives and the loftiest ideals. This made me create a new ethical atmosphere and the refined thinking of ethical imperatives by means of a gracious spirit, but all these are the direct outcome of God's good Personality and his spiritual journey of hope. I say unto you, the sphere of morals is faith. I have, indeed, been taken for granted; but as far as I have observed, they have not directly based God's good morals upon his spiritual teachings, and yet it is the one thing that is most obvious.

I should frankly state that it has been my chief endeavour to end the games false friends played in my social life and to prove that social progress is dependent upon the high ethics of my Christian faith. The more carefully I read my own journey of hope through the lens of philosophy and watch the social outcome, the more I am convinced that the games are over. I have faced adversity many a time, and through determination and courage, indeed, on occasion, blind faith, I've managed to overcome such adversity (as far as anyone really ever can), and, I believe, have carved a humbly successful life.

It also shows how necessary it is to use the lessons I've learnt on my life's path so far, those I draw on, to create the books I've previously written, which are related to economic problems that demand a solution that cannot be delayed on my journey of hope. When this journey of hope is sympathetically undertaken, the direct bearing of the game on social life becomes immediately apparent and evokes interest.

However, since commerce operates worldwide and economic principles are universal, and, further, since mankind is a brotherhood, we must bear upon international life in all its aspects. I have shown that the moral law, applicable to individuals and to the family life, can also regulate life. It calls loudly for attention.

With this book, as before, I reflect on the experiences and challenges of my life, using them to demonstrate how such experiences can be used positively by others to help mould and improve life as it moves forward.

It also carries with it a healing and elevating influence. Because it is at once tender and strong, beautiful and mighty, those who profess to obey its dictates must take wide and long views of life. I must be careful as to the agencies I select in order to give it expression in this book; however, I have decided to also pull upon the experiences of others. It is that which interprets, and likewise illumines, life. But it is not to be connected with any political party. It may give inspiration and direction to politics, but, rightly understood, it cannot be made identical with any political party for each of us are unique, and each of us, at some point in our lives, will face challenges, dishonesty and betrayal. Some, unfortunately, feel these difficulties more than others.

However, the key to moving forward is often in the way in which we view these challenges and difficulties. Therefore, the spirit to which the journey of hope owes allegiance cannot be mistaken, nor can the duties of this spirit to end the games be misunderstood. Seeing class war, hatred, a passion for material things and the neglect of spiritual development tries to destroy my spirit of hope.

If we see that these experiences can help us to grow, to learn, to have drive and determination to succeed, then such challenges and misfortunes can be turned around and can act as stepping stones to success.

Although these are sometimes falsely offered by some people, they are foreign to the resolve that the games are over. I believe it is only because of my passion for loving people and the goodwill of God righteousness that my journey of hope has allowed me to forgive the wrongs that have been done to me. My journey of hope and the search for the truth has taught me a lot and I can affirm the game is truly over and I am back in my rightful place.

Several months ago, I launched my second semi-autobiographical book, entitled *Standing in Pain—Stronger than before*. I am under a debt of gratitude to my true friends whom I will not name, for their kind reading, and I gladly acknowledge the service they rendered while the work was passing through the press. The launch was attended by friends and family members who wanted to share in my personal success and enjoy the occasion with me. Book launches are funny affairs. The build-up and the planning of a launch can be overwhelming because of the desire to create a relaxed and enjoyable environment resting solely on the author's shoulders.

All who read and observe are aware that a persistent and fierce attack was made upon my business, left me in pain, but, sometime later, I came out stronger than before. The assault is thus directed not at one point only, but at every place where it seems the assailants the walls of the citadel may be scaled by my journey of good hope. The fact of the assault is not the journey of hope but the stopper of my journey of hope, however, is the only thing that deserves attention. In addition, it must be noted that the most powerful weapons that ingenuity can devise are skilfully and persistently employed from the Holy Bible in Ephesians Chapter 6, which reads, 'For we wrestle not against flesh and blood, but against principalities, against powers, against the rulers of the darkness of this world, against spiritual wickedness in high places' (Ephesians 6: 12 KJV).

How the assault is conducted leaves me standing in pain and not without interest. However, one cannot resist an interjection of surprise now and again while one watches the operations of the assailants. This is how they proceed. Their further allegations have undermined my business, and now, they say, a fine ear can hear the creaking and straining of the falling timbers of my business edifice, which made me stronger today.

Then of course there is the hope that attendees will enjoy the book I've spent months, sometimes years working on. And you want them to really, truthfully enjoy it—to learn and gain from it. This, after all, is the marker of a successful book. If others enjoy, if others learn, then the book almost instantaneously renders itself worthwhile. With such worry and desire and hope comes the relief of having finally finished the book. A book launch marks that very moment when you turn the book away from your hands and into the hands of the readers. This picture of desolation is complete. It was painted in dark colours. There is not even a streak of light in it to cheer and encourage from some. All this is dismal and forbidding.

One might say at once that, where justification was found for this picture of desolation, one should bid farewell to long cherished hopes that the games are over. But what of the message of righteousness? Which people, inspired by the Christian faith, have often thundered the teaching of the Bible in the ears of morally decadent nations? This made me think from the beginning of these people's journey of hope to a new spiritual and moral life.

CHAPTER 1
Why do we have Enemies?

Over the past few years, I've found that I finally have the time and life experiences needed to write, and write about something that is at least semi-meaningful. I've had a colourful life, one driven by a desire to achieve, to support my family and those around me and, importantly for me, to follow a good, Christian life. The path of life I've followed has not always been smooth or well supported. I have faced adversity many a time, and not wanting to surrender to it , and indeed on occasion blind faith, I've managed to overcome such adversity (as far as anyone really ever can) and, I believe, have carved a humbly successful life. It is the lessons I've learnt along my life's path thus far that I've utilised to create the books I've previously written. With this book, as before, I reflect on the experiences and challenges of my life, using them to demonstrate how such experiences can be used positively by others to help mould and improve life as it moves forward.

In this book however, I have decided to also draw upon the experiences of others. For each of us are unique, and each of us, at some point in our lives, will face challenges, will face dishonestly and betrayal. Some unfortunately feel these difficulties more than others. But the key to moving forward is often in the way in which we view these challenges and difficulties. If we see that these experiences can help us to grow, to learn and to have the drive and determination to succeed, then such challenges and misfortunes can be turned around and can act as the stepping stones to success.

Several months ago, I launched my second semi-autobiographical book, entitled *Standing in Pain—Stronger than before*. The launch was attended by friends and family members who wanted to share in my personal success and enjoy the occasion with me. Book launches are funny affairs. The build-up and the planning of a launch can be overwhelming because the desire to create a relaxed and enjoyable environment rests solely on the author's shoulders. Then, of course, there is the hope that attendees will enjoy the book you've spent months, sometimes years working on, and you want them to really, truthfully enjoy it, to learn and gain from it. This, after all, is the marker of a successful book. If others enjoy, if others learn, then the book almost instantaneously renders itself worthwhile. With such worry and desire and hope comes the relief of having finally finished the book. A book launch marks that very moment when you turn the book away from your hands and into the hands of the readers.

For me, the launch of *Standing in Pain—Stronger Than Before* was everything I could have hoped for. Enthusiastic family members and friends gathered to toast the book that had taken me months to complete. I gladly moved the book into their hands, eager for them to read, to learn and to enjoy.

Following the launch a good friend of mine, Christina, invited me to join her in a café in central London. She'd been absent from the book launch and wanted to celebrate my success in a small way over coffee and patisseries at one of her favourite coffee houses. Possessing a love for anything sweet and of course for good company, I gladly accepted.

Over coffee and cake, I relived the launch for her, talking her through the guest list, the room in which the book had been launched, the speeches, the gaiety of the celebrations in general. Christina listened acutely; always keen to be involved, even from afar. We then spoke a little about the experiences I'd recounted in my book and the content of the book in general. As a semi-autobiographical book, the focus of our discussions was predominately directed towards me: my life, my stories, my hardship, my belief in a greater good, and indeed my quest to find it. Talking about me is not something that comes naturally—let's be honest; most people find themselves to be a difficult topic of conversation. Therefore, at the earliest opportunity, I began to swing the conversation away from my personal story and towards that of Christina. I felt that Christina wanted to share her personal experiences with me in the same way that I'd openly shared mine with the world, but she held back, so I didn't push the subject. We moved onto general, meaningless chatter and our meeting naturally came to an end.

'Lunch?' she suggested suddenly, as I hugged her goodbye.

'Of course', I agreed warmly, 'when were you thinking?'

'Saturday?'

'Sounds great. Shall I bring Faye?'

'Yes, please do. I'd love to meet her properly'.

'Great. I'll meet you here at 11 a.m. and then we can go on and find somewhere to eat. If the weather holds, perhaps we can take a stroll along the embankment'.

'I'll look forward to it', Christina smiled before signalling a little goodbye and turning to walk towards the nearest tube station.

Faye couldn't join us that Saturday morning; the social calendars of our children tend to dictate our weekends, and she needed to spend the time taking one to a sports class and the other to a friend's house. So I met with Christina alone.

We walked through St James' Park to a little Italian bistro I've frequented for several years now. The smell of the garlic oil and cooked mozzarella cheese hits you as soon as you walk through the doors; it is a comforting smell, one which cocoons you with safety and ease. We took a table near the window so that people watching would be easy if the moment ever called for it. It was also the most secluded table, and I felt as if Christina wanted to talk privately with me that afternoon; she'd appeared almost purposeful in manner all morning.

It didn't take long for Christina to offload. It quickly became apparent that she'd suffered betrayal, cruelty and heartbreak in the way I also had.

'I have to confess Peter that I have always been a tolerant person, just like you. I have overlooked things in life that maybe I should have been more careful of.'

'Go on', I prompted encouragingly.

She pondered for a moment and then said, 'we are exposed to certain people who use and plan strategies to cover up their devilish ways. They do this by trying cunningly to pull, even drag nice and kind people down, yet, even with their well-planned tactics, sometimes something inside of you leads you to feel sorry for them.

'For example, you'd expect a mother to bring together her squabbling children, encouraging them to make peace with each other, wouldn't you? But for children who are so obviously excluded from their mother's love, it is just impossible for them to be peacefully included in the family unit. Why would a mother deliberately divide or segregate her children in this way?'

I guessed this to be a rhetorical question, so just shrugged my shoulders in quiet agreement.

'I remember a time back when I was pregnant with my first child. It was a very cold winter's day, and I knew that the night to follow would be much colder. I headed off to a relative's house to ask to borrow an extra blanket to keep myself and my unborn child warm that night. Well, I will never forget the sick feeling I had inside me when I was refused. I cried all the way back home I was so distraught.

'That day really opened my eyes and showed me how cruel the people around us can be at times. There was no reason for her to refuse to lend me a blanket. We were family—I'd done nothing to her, nothing to the family that could ever justify such an attitude. I can only assume that she resented me somehow and in some unspoken way. Funny how resentment always seems to manifest its ugly head when we least expect it too'.

I was shocked by the story Christina had imparted. There could be no excuse for such behaviour—none. Yet, I knew the suffering and humiliation she'd felt all too well, for I too had suffered from the powers of resentment. My aim is to build a successful business. I have no knowledge that people around me, friends and many relatives resented that and had turned against me. They had become angry and resentful towards me. Yet all I wanted was to be a success and share my achievements with them.

Christina, like me, had a Christian faith that had kept her strong.

'I knew then', she continued, 'that I would empower myself with all the knowledge God had intended me to have. I was determined that I would have made something of myself the next time I saw them.'

'I admire your determination and ambition Christina, I really do. And you did it! You are a success—you have a strong career, a wonderful family. You did make something of yourself'.

Our starters arrived and we tucked in heartedly. Silently we ate; hungry from our initial discussions.

'The difficulty is', Christina continued between mouthfuls, 'others are rarely happy or proud of another person's success. Even when you do feel that you've made something of yourself, those closest to you are there, quick to criticise and highlight your faults, always believing that they can do everything so much better than you ever could'.

I thought for a moment and then responded. 'I think the key is in recognising what actually counts as success. Success isn't necessarily fame and fortune and wealth. Unless you can determine what success is for you personally, you can waste an awful lot of time chasing the future—believing it to hold the key to your happiness—when actually your happiness and indeed success lies in what sits in front of you. For me that's family, love, laughter and friends'.

Christina's eyes welled a little, and I worried momentarily that I'd upset her in some way.

'But that's exactly my point Peter', she spluttered. 'It has taken me until now to realise that I was wrong. These past few years I've been driven to succeed financially and to be able to demonstrate my success to those who never believed in me through the physical display of wealth. All I've found is that they want to criticise me, and then abuse my success and my generosity when it suits them. I've spent so much time trying to please everyone and in turn have neglected to pursue what it is that I really and truly want—what I believe will act as the key to my success and to my happiness. And that is to enjoy my children, my friends and my life and to stop chasing every career opportunity and instead ground myself in my family life. I can't believe it has taken me so long to realise that I got life so very wrong. The old saying goes "If you think everyone is good, and then you have not met everyone".' Christina quoted the following passage below from the bible which she had often recited:

'That ye may be the children of your Father which is in heaven: for He maketh his sun to rise on the evil and on the good, and sendeth rain on the just and on the unjust' (Matthew 5:45KJV).

'But you have realised', I murmured compassionately, 'and you've still so much time for action and refocus. You're children are still small, you have a husband who adores you and good friends. Nothing has been wasted—nothing lost. Embrace this epiphany and enjoy the life path you've decided to follow'.

And with that I raised a glass. Christina lifted hers in response and smiled.

'To new beginnings and enjoying lessons learnt', she smiled.

'Yes indeed', I laughed as our glasses clinked.

As I strolled home that afternoon, my lunch with Christina led me to think about jealously. The last few years of Christina's life had been taken up with trying to prove that she was worthy and then being knocked down and in many ways, emotionally and financially abused by the very people she was working to impress. What is perhaps even more shocking is the realisation that it is her family that led her to believe that she was anything other than worthy, and her family chose to dismiss and diminish her success unless they could find a way to make that success beneficial to themselves. What lay at the centre of this behaviour was jealously.

Life is complicated. Everyone is in a race to get to the top. I believe there needs to be a balance between good and evil. In addition, if life were always easy and always fair, what fun would it be? Besides, not everyone is compatible. People have different views, ideas and religions. Our belief systems are different, so it is inevitable that we won't always understand one another. In any case, a perfect life is an imperfect life. I use the word 'evil' here because people need to feel that they are better than someone else; without enemies, people wouldn't know how to change themselves to be a better person. They use the enemy to make sure they are not like that person and then make life better for themselves. Having enemies keeps us focused because we always have to try not to fall flat in front of those enemies.

'Owe no man anything, but to love one another: for he that loveth another hath fulfilled the law' (Romans 13:8 KJV).

I was once told to listen to my enemies; I asked why I should and was told, 'because your enemies will be first to point out your faults'.

'God left him to test him and to know everything that was in his heart' (2 Chronicles 32:31 KJV).

When Jesus said, 'Love your enemies', he assumed that there'd be more than one enemy in individual's lives, and most people do find more than one enemy throughout their life. Sadly, many, if not all of us, will find that one or more of our enemies rest within—it could be a sibling, another family, a friend or even a community of faith. Certainly, Jesus assumed this and nothing has really changed since. Much persecution and evil doing comes from those who claim to believe in God as much as we all do. Yet, the issues between you may not be theological. Your enemy may simply not like you purely because you are, in their eyes, more successful than them. For example, your enemy may just not be able to cope with the person you've become or perhaps they disagree with your stance on a particular question or issue. Many may find that they do not understand why people they like or love have suddenly become their enemies, and this is because this shift in behaviour is usually through no fault of their own.

Have you ever thought that those so-called jealous people may be angry with God for blessing you or for putting you where you are?

They could well be. You have that prestigious job. It pays well. You are admired by your boss and the people in your office. God has blessed you with certain talents and gifts. There will always be someone who will be jealous and seek to bring you down. If you have been blessed with a good reputation, do not be surprised if someone resents it. Unfortunately, your enemy doesn't know that he or she is probably actually angry with God.

The ultimate reason you and I have an enemy is that it fits God's purpose. Why? It is what we need. It helps to humble us lest we take ourselves too seriously. An enemy shows us what we are like.

So don't be angry with your enemy! It is God who is at work on your heart!

Each individual has their unique star from The Almighty God and he knows each star by name. Just like our parents give us a name, and our name depicts our unique identity to them.

Remember, if the stars are brighter than the moon that is the work of God. Who can stop the work of God? Within your work or whatsoever you are doing, do it to the best of your ability. We should be grateful to God, for God will only give us things that we can handle.

There are many people who try to hide behind God and the church as a means of masking their jealously and the destructive nature this jealously brings. I am a strong Christian. I believe in following the principles of the Bible. However, I am acutely aware that interpretation of religion itself is the cause of many battles, many wars, the division of families and the ending of relationships. It is not religion itself that causes such behaviour, but the way in which individuals interpret the content of the religious teachings.

Therefore, it is hardly surprising that the church can be an easy place for those with impure hearts to hide. At a church that I used to attend, for example, there was an elderly lady who held an established and clear role within the functioning of the church, and she was a regular church goer. However, I understood that she'd spent a lifetime inflicting pain on other family members. Her joy seemed to come from suppressing the people within her circle of family and friends by working to ensure that they never did better than her. How can such actions possibly marry up with the teachings of the Christian religion? They don't. And so her time to fall will come. As the Bible says, 'A virtuous woman is a crown to her husband: but she that maketh ashamed is as rottenness in his bones' (Proverbs 12:4 KJV).

Similarly, I know a man he cares for nothing but himself. He could never be a role model to anyone or set a good example. He spends his time constantly trying to undermine people and is always waiting in the background for something to happen so he can portion blame and point a finger. As the Bible says, 'But if any provide not for his own, and especially for those of his own house, he hath denied the faith, and is worse than an infidel'(1 Timothy 5:8 KJV).

If he were as wise as he tries to portray to people, he would spend more time keeping an eye on his own family. Then maybe they would not have turned out to be so dysfunctional. But jealously of others has led him to follow a more destructive path.

We all have examples of individuals who have acted immorally through jealously. The key is to recognise this behaviour and to not rise to the challenges they seem to continually place on us. Instead, keep hold of what is important to you, remember how you personally define success and happiness and continue to pursue these areas as you navigate through life.

'For my thoughts are not your thoughts, neither are your ways my ways, saith the LORD. For as the heavens are higher than the earth, so are my ways higher than your ways, and my thoughts than your thoughts' (Isaiah 55:8-9 KJV).

CHAPTER 2
Jealousy and Envy

In Chapter 1, we looked at examples of how individuals, and importantly family members, can belittle, cause harm or even abuse others, purely because they are jealous of the perceived life and successes of the targeted individual. This behaviour, particularly when carried out by those who are supposed to feel nothing but warmth and love for the victim, seems inexcusable. It is, however, all too frequently seen.

Within this second chapter, I believe it is necessary to look at other groups of individuals who can cause pain to those they 'should' love, respect and care for. Perhaps the most logical place to start is with friends.

From a very young age, we all learn some of the painful lessons that are associated with the formation of friendships. Friends can be very loyal, kind and loving and in many instances a friendship is as strong as (or stronger than) family ties. They can, however, backfire. In the playground, friendships are easily formed and easily discarded. Others come along and are perceived as being more interesting, cooler, sportier than the best friend that was before. There is also the natural breakdown of friendships, where people naturally move on and away from those who were so important to them moments before. These lessons can be hard to swallow at the time, particularly for children or young people who feel, at that precise moment, as if their world has been blown apart by the loss of a friend. However, as we all know, everyone heals from such losses, and we all go on to form different and potentially more significant relationships and friendships over time.

Such breakdowns in friendship are natural, normal and to be expected throughout life. They are very different from the sabotaging of an individual through selfish motives or immoral values. The natural termination of relationships, or the flitting between friendships that children often display, are actions that are not driven by malicious behaviour or a drive to cause pain to another. It is those actions that deliberately hurt others with which this chapter deals.

'Let us not be desirous of vain glory, provoking one another, envying one' (Galatians 5:26 KJV).

In order to explore the theme of hurt caused by 'friends' or false friendships, I shall start by discussing a personal example that I encountered whilst a young adult in my latter school days.

Whilst at school, I formed a friendship with a boy named Nicholas. Nicholas was five years older than me, and, to be honest, I was thrilled to have been 'chosen' to be one of his friends, to be allowed into his inner sanctum and to be able to form a relationship with him. I felt that I would learn a lot from an individual who took an interest in my life and had five years of life experience that I hadn't yet encountered.

My family, however, was not particularly supportive of my friendship with Nicholas. My father and my uncle specifically warned me on several occasions that

Nicholas was a shifty character who didn't display even an ounce of ambition or drive to build a future for himself. They were nervous of him, and they were nervous of his influence over me. Given my age, however, my family couldn't ban me from holding a friendship with someone I admired. They just presented me with their concerns and told me that they hoped they'd be proven wrong and that Nicholas wouldn't be destructive in the way they felt sure he would be. I, of course, was determined to prove them wrong and so strove ahead with our friendship. It didn't take too long for the words of warning from my elders to come back and haunt me; their concerns were indeed well founded.

'Listen to advice and accept instruction, that you may gain wisdom in the future' (Proverbs 19:20 ESV).

A pattern started to emerge. Whenever I was with other friends, Nicholas would tell me that these friends were no good for me. He would make up lies about their behaviour and character and discourage my friendship with them. I valued his opinion, so I would eventually break away from each of my existing friendships.

'Whoever walks with the wise becomes wise, but the companion of fools will suffer harm' (Proverbs 13:20 ESV).

I should have been able to see this pattern, to recognise that Nicholas was systematically trying to destroy my friendships. My other friends, people I'd had relationships with for a long time, were upset by my behaviour and tried to get me to see the negative influence Nicholas was having on my life. But I didn't see it until it was too late.

'A heart at peace gives life to the body, but envy rots the bones' (Proverbs 14:30 ESV).

You might see this sort of behaviour in so-called friendships that have held, hold or will hold in the future. Or you might witness another form of negative behaviour brought on by someone who you believed to be a friend—an individual who might look to sabotage your family relationships for example, or may talk negatively about you with others or may look to claim credit and glory from work that you have created or successes you have attained. There are lots of examples of negative behaviour that friends can display intentionally in order to cause you some pain or harm. Whilst the intention for such action may never be disclosed publicly by your 'friend', remember that generally speaking, it is jealously that brings about such behaviour.

So why do people become jealous of others?

Jealousy is one of those demons that seem to take everything over when it is felt—even when an individual knows on the inside that their jealousy doesn't make sense, somehow it often still rips through and takes that person hostage. Many people even go so far as to call jealousy an innate emotion, as though, no matter what, we will always feel some jealousy sometimes, and there's nothing we can do to help that. That may be true, but jealously becomes difficult when it is acted upon instead of simply acknowledged as a feeling, put to one side, and overcome.

How do envy and jealousy differ?

Envy happens when you see somebody else experiencing something you'd like to have. You get a wishful feeling inside, like you want what they have. But this feeling does not necessarily lead to jealousy; you can be envious of somebody's situation yet still admire them. For example, say one of your friends is doing a workout routine and is in really good shape. You envy them, and you come up to them and ask their secret or maybe if you can join them and do what they do. This is an example of an envious response that leads not to jealousy, but rather to motivating, progressive thinking.

Pure jealousy, however, is different; it is an altogether negative, regressive state of mind. The jealous thought says, 'I want what you have, and thus until I have it, you shouldn't have it either'. This is very different from simple envy because now the emphasis is not on the individual moving forward, but rather on keeping the other person back. That's why jealousy can be so destructive and all-consuming; the jealous individual gets into a state of mind that presumes the right to control other people's pleasure.

Little feelings of jealousy are understandable sometimes and can be controlled. We all recognise times when we acted or thought badly of another due to our own selfish standpoint. Most of us repent (sometimes to God) following displays of this behaviour and learn to adjust our behaviour or thought processes in the future. However, chronic jealousy comes from a perspective of self-preservation, not through a perspective of love towards others. Let's look at why that is.

Where are jealous feelings rooted?

Often the force of jealousy comes from the feeling that you are about to lose something because it will be shared, or, by sharing it, you are in danger of losing it. Aversion to loss is quite natural. Of course, even people who feel no jealousy also have times when they fear losing something precious. It's part of the human experience. An aversion to loss, however, is not an excuse for jealous behaviour or for the actions that usually accompany jealousy.

Jealously for another person is often rooted in the fact that individuals believe a person to be their 'property' and thus the 'owner' can control and manipulate them. Take the example of myself and Nicholas. Nicholas believed that I was his property, and he could dictate and control how I spent my time, who I socialised with and the other relationships I formed. In reality, an individual cannot control how another person feels or what they want, but, through the power of jealously, they may try.

What is important to remember is that jealous individuals do exist, and we all will, at some point in our life, encounter individuals who want to betray us, fuelled by their jealousy, no matter how committed to a friendship with us they might at first appear. The key is to be able to recognise these individuals and, as hard as it may seem, break away from them or look to find a way to support them come to terms with their jealous tendencies, without falling victim to their behaviour.

Remember, everyday life gives us an opportunity to do something meaningful and positive for ourselves and for others; it is up to us to decide whether to grasp this opportunity or not.

As the Bible says, 'Let no corrupting talk come out of your mouths, but only such as is good for building up, as fits the occasion, that it may give grace to those who hear. And do not grieve the Holy Spirit of God, by whom you were sealed for the day of redemption. Let all bitterness and wrath and anger and clamour and slander be put away from you, along with all malice. Be kind to one another, tender hearted, forgiving one another, as God in Christ forgave you' (Ephesians 4:29-32 ESV).

CHAPTER 3
Power - its Positive and Negative Aspects

Throughout Chapters 1 and 2, we explored the reasons why some individuals cause pain to their loved ones, focusing on both family and friend relationships. The conclusion made within this topic was that jealousy often fuels spiteful and hurtful action.

One area that is related to this idea is that of power.

To possess power and control over others has both a positive and negative aspect. We must always hope that it is used to generate the good from people rather than evil. We do, however, live in an imperfect world and so there are many occasions where power can be abused and used in a negative way that can be both detrimental to an individual and to a cause in general. It is important to remember that power isn't always permanent. An individual may believe they hold power and are untouchable, but power can be taken away. When it is, the consequences of the once 'powerful' individual can be grave.

Let's first take a look at the concept of 'power' in general and then move on to consider how it can and should be used positively.

Power is everywhere
Power operates both negatively and positively at many levels, in public and private, in the workplace, market and family, in relations with friends and colleagues and

even at a very personal level within each individual. On the negative side, as we've already suggested, it can work to prevent people's participation and the fulfilment of their rights, and, on the positive, it can serve as a source of strength to promote their involvement and struggle for justice.

We need to look beyond the notion that power operates almost exclusively in the public sphere of governments and political parties or in conflicts between capital and labour (employers versus workers, small farmers and peasants versus plantation owners). Gender relations, for example, show us how power plays out in the private sphere of family and personal relationships and how it affects women's ability to participate and become active agents of change.

Different ways of understanding power

As we've alluded to above, generally speaking, power is thought of in a negative sense. The concept of 'power over' someone or something is seen to be negative and, when used in this way, can be detrimental to the individual who is seen as the 'repressed'.

But there are alternative and more positive ways in which power can be considered, and if we are to take the concept of utilising power in a positive way (a path that needs to be taken and should be taken by anyone aware of the fact that the power they hold could indeed be lost at any given point), then these are definitions that should be praised:

Power to act: The unique potential of every person and social group to shape their life and world and create more equitable relationships and structures of power

Power within ourselves: People's sense of self-worth, values and self-knowledge as central to individual and group understanding of being citizens with rights and responsibilities

Power with others: Finding common ground among different interests and building collective strength to challenge injustice

How to use power positively

Almost everyone will at some point in their life realise that they have the potential to hold power over something or someone, and that, within a relationship; it is they who have a greater level of influence or control. The following example demonstrates nicely how this could be the case and how individuals may find themselves repressed through the power of one particular individual, then find that they are repressing another person at the same time.

> A small farmer or peasant living in utter poverty is vulnerable to the authority, power and sometimes violence of vast estate owners and multinational agribusiness. Yet this same farmer may establish an authoritarian and violent relationship with the women and female

members of his family since he is immersed in a patriarchal and macho culture.[1]

So, with us all able to access power at some point in our lives, strategies are needed to ensure that power is used positively, not negatively or in a way that is repressive.

John Samuel, working with campaign staff in Bangkok in 2004, outlined five underlying notions related to the values and principles of 'good' individuals, which can be integrated into the way we think of and use power:

1. **Rights:** Human rights and related values of social justice are the guiding principles that shape our vision and exercise of power. They provide the basis to energise and mobilise people, especially the poor and excluded, so they can advance and exercise their rights in all dimensions of their lives with integrity.
2. **Democracy:** By tapping positive forms of power (especially power to/within/with) and collaborating with groups or individuals who have been excluded, we can all work to develop more democratic and inclusive structures and processes.

---

[1] www.civitas.edu.pl

3. **Social Justice:** Gaining power is not an end in itself, but a means to fight for social justice and, by so doing, develop more equitable, caring and supportive human relationships.
4. **Solidarity:** If we were all to reflect on the potential negative impact that power can have and indeed the manner in which these negatives can be re-addressed to bring about positive change, then such reflections should encourage us to develop a perspective and agenda that goes beyond our own specific advocacy issues.
5. **Respect for difference:** No matter how much power you may believe yourself to have and to utilise, even in a positive manner, it is important to remember that others will disagree with you at times and that their opinion matters even if, ultimately, you choose to act in a way that goes against their views. Respecting differences in opinion and values is important when using power, no matter what the cause or potential gain.

No position is permanent

As we've explored in the sections above, each of us can and will hold power at some point in our life; and the majority possess such power all of the time, just to different degrees and within different relationships. It is important to remember that relationships change and move with the wind; they are never permanent, thus the power that is found within a relationship can change, bend and snap very quickly. The quote below, from Mumia Abu-Jamal sums up this concept nicely;

> What history really shows is that today's empire is tomorrow's ashes, that nothing lasts forever, and that to not resist is to acquiesce in your own oppression. The greatest form of sanity that anyone can exercise is to resist that force that is trying to repress, oppress, and fight down the human spirit (Mumia Abu Jamal).

Power, respect and love
I believe that using power in a positive way is a concept that is intrinsically linked with respectful behaviour and love. We earn respect by the way we conduct ourselves, and we are loved by others for the way we convey respect towards them. By using authority respectfully, we allow ourselves to be loved, to love, and to demonstrate respect. This links us back to the five principles of using power in a positive way that are outlined above; rights, democracy, social justice, solidarity and respecting differences.

As a Christian, I believe that when God puts someone in a position of leadership he presents them with many opportunities. The aim here is to make the right choices that will promote equality and fairness which can be use wisely in a satisfying and acknowledged way. The power here is positive. The outcome is positive. And the outcome is driven through love and respect of others.

As the Bible says:

> Understand, ye brutish among the people: and ye fools, when will ye be wise? He that planted the ear, shall he not hear? He that formed the eye, shall he not see? He that chastiseth the heathen, shall not he correct? He that teacheth man knowledge, shall not he know? The LORD knoweth the thoughts of man, that they are vanity. (Psalm 94:8-11, KJV)

CHAPTER 4
God, Present Everywhere

In Chapter 1 of this book, I spoke about a friend of mine, Christina, and the difficulties she'd experienced with her family. She'd seen, as I have, that her own personal success or her determination for success led to members of her very own family being jealous of her and acting in a way that was detrimental to her, her good nature and indeed her well-being.

I have also experienced such attitudes from those I love; there have been times when I heard relatives of mine discussing my family and me, criticising and laughing about things we have done. I couldn't understand what wrong I had done to them, how could what I was doing for my future and that of my family affect them in that way? I could only surmise that such discussion was born through jealous—a topic we've discussed in the first three chapters of this book.

In all chapters, I have alluded to the importance of securing faith in God when you find yourself criticised or hurt by individuals with whom you thought you had a positive relationship. Whilst it can be reassuring to remember that the power and hurtful comments made about you by these individuals are generally created through jealous behaviour, having an understanding of the background of negative actions isn't always sufficient when it comes to overcoming the pain caused by others. On occasions such as this, there is a need to turn to God, to have faith in God and to remember that he is all seeing and all-knowing and that through faith you will reap the benefits of the life you have been driven to create.

In Jeremiah 23:24, God asks, 'Do I not fill heaven and earth?' God is present in all places. His spirit is everywhere—in heaven, on earth and in hell. Although such a concept may surpass the understanding of creatures like us, who are limited and bound to material bodies, God is present everywhere in His majesty and power.

God is omnipotent, which means that the totality of his essence, without diffusion or expansion, multiplication or division, penetrates and fills the universe and beyond. Let's remember then that if God is present in the earth,

- He is essentially present in all places,
- He is essentially present at all times,
- He is essentially present with all creatures,
- His essential presence is without any division of Himself,
- His presence is not a multiplication of Himself,
- He is thus totally everywhere by his own simple substance.[2]

A story about a man called Joseph and his two sons demonstrates how such a strong belief in God and in the power of God can be instilled in children from a

---

[2] www.tecmalta.org/tft138.htm

young age. By doing so, their resilience and tolerance to jealous can be built, and their reactions towards others when they themselves feel pangs of jealousy can be shaped to enable them to respond in a positive and kind way.

Joseph has faith in God and teaches his two sons the same faith. He tells his two sons that God is everywhere.

Joseph lectures his two sons, Alexander and Gabriel, about the importance of being truthful and honest, of the need to attend church to worship and to pay your vows to the church. Joseph tells his children that the deceiver's ultimate victim is always himself. He reinforces the importance of telling the truth, for truth is like oil, no matter how much water you pour on it, it will always float.

One Sunday morning, Alexander and Gabriel get themselves ready to go to church, and their father gives them money to give to the church in order to pay their vows and to buy their Sunday breakfast. The elder of the two boys, Alexander, decides that it would be a good idea to have a game of football with his young brother Gabriel and some friends before proceeding to church. Unfortunately, Gabriel loses part of his money whilst playing football. Gabriel tells Alexander that he's lost part of his during the football game. Alexander replies to Gabriel that he shouldn't worry, for 'God is everywhere'.

Both Alexander and Gabriel proceed to church, and when the time approaches for them to pay their vows, Gabriel reminds Alexander that he only has enough money left for breakfast and no money to put forward for the church vow.

Alexander instructs Gabriel to pay his vow. 'But if God is everywhere', says Gabriel, 'he would have seen that I lost the money that I had ready for Him whilst playing football'.

Alexander continues to instruct Gabriel to put the money he has forward for the church.

Gabriel fears aloud, 'If I give my money to the church, I'll have no money for breakfast!'

Alexander smiles at Gabriel and states that God will provide as long he has faith. 'Remember that God see everything and knows everything—he knows that you lost your money whilst playing football—and that such an action was accidental. He will also now see that you have passed all of the money you do have to the church—potentially sacrificing your own breakfast to give to others. Such behaviour will not go un-noticed. With faith in God, you will have breakfast this morning'.

So faith can enable you to act selflessly even when you fear the repercussions to your well-being. Such positive action contrasts drastically with the negative, jealous reaction that can be seen by others who do not hold the belief that God is everywhere close to their hearts.

God's omnipresence is neglected by many and forgotten by more. Some people may pretend to believe that God is present everywhere, but they then go on to live as if He is non-existent or absent from their day-to-day lives. These individuals, as we've discussed in previous chapters, can fall into many vain conceits, plan their extravagant projects, and endeavour to fulfil their ambitions, all because they wilfully forgot that God is everywhere. He is there looking upon the godliness of the wise and the foolishness of the wicked.[3]

'In their lost condition men forget, not to say deny, this divine attribute. Like our first parents, they hide in the trees of the garden, supposedly to avoid the presence of God. Thus further and further sin is spawned'.[4]

As we work through day-to-day life, there are many reasons to rejoice and take heart from the omnipotent presence of God. As we've discussed, the fact that God is everywhere can give us the strength to rise above the injustice afforded us by others, particularly when such injustice or conceit is directed by those we believed loved and cherished us. In addition, belief in the continuous presence of God can spur on honest, loving and positive behaviour towards others and thus help to tackle the negativities of jealousy. Let's summarise some of the key reasons for taking strengthen and joy from God's omnipresence, ESV:

1. God's omnipresence is a shield against all temptations—'Moses beheld Him who is invisible, and this strengthened him against the costly pleasures and luxuries of a prince's court' (Hebrews 11:27).

---

[3] www.tecmalta.org/tft138.htm
[4] www.tecmalta.org/tft138.htm

2. God's omnipresence is a spur to holy actions—'Every good gift and every perfect gift is from above, coming down from the Father of lights with whom there is no variation or shadow due to change' (James 17:1).
3. God's omnipresence, carefully considered, will remove distractions in worship—'In all ways acknowledge Him, and He shall direct thy paths' (Proverbs 3:6).
4. The divine omnipresence is a comfort in all violent temptations—'Yea, though I walk through the valley of the shadow of death, I will fear no evil; for thou art with me; thy rod and thy staff they comfort me' (Psalms 23:4).
5. His all-seeing and all-knowing presence is a comfort in sharp afflictions—'When my father and mother forsake me, then the Lord shall take me up' (Psalms 27:10).
6. God is a present help in trouble—'God is our refuge and strength, a very present help in trouble. Therefore, we will not fear though the earth gives way, though the mountains be moved into the heart of the sea, though its waters roar and foam, though the mountains tremble at its swelling. Selah There is a river whose streams make glad the city of God, the holy habitation of the Most High. 'God is in the midst of her; she shall not be moved; God will help her when morning dawns' (Psalms 46:1-6).

7. The omnipotent presence of God is a comfort in all duties of worship—'By which he has granted to us his precious and very great promises, so that through them you may become partakers of the divine nature, having escaped from the corruption that is in the world because of sinful desire' (2 Peter1:4).

We should all take the time to believe, and to truly believe, that He is with us always, for if more of us acted in such a way, then people would certainly be more obedient, more dedicated to the cause of His everlasting kingdom.

CHAPTER 5
Kindness for Weakness

Over the last few years, I have looked back at so many events in my life and have considered how people can and, often have, taken the notion of an individual's kindness for a weakness. Generosity can also be considered a weakness. This I mentioned in my book, entitled *From the bottom to the Top Volume Two.* It seems to me that if we are to believe that generosity is a weakness, then we will by default create an unequal relationship between ourselves and our fellow man, he whom we supposedly wish to help, for I truly believe that the very act of helping, or giving, should make us better or more blessed people.

As Bible says, 'In all things I have shown you that by working hard in this way we must help the weak and remember the words of the Lord Jesus, how he himself said, "It is more blessed to give than to receive"' (Acts 20:35 ESV).

A great and practical example of the importance of sharing your generosity and of ensuring that you never give to receive can be seen on the sharing of occasional gifts. On occasions such as birthdays, anniversaries, Christmas etc., it is important to remember that the act of giving is just that—an act in itself that does not need the same level of thought or generosity returned. As important a lesson as this is, there are some people who think it is their right to receive and even demand to receive something specific. Indeed, when these individuals do receive, they generally never appreciate the gift they've actually been given.

I believe that we should all take time to reflect on how the person who gave us our present feels, and what they went through to be able to purchase or provide the present in the first place. Personally, this level of reflection often makes it difficult for me to be able to open up myself to receive.

Sometimes in life, we learn through experiences of things that have occurred to us or that we have heard or read about. I remember how a friend once mentioned that his friend had given his son some money. However, my friend felt that the amount of money he'd given his son was insufficient, for he knew how much money the man held; because of this he judged his generosity as insufficient.

The question here looks at whether his friend should have felt compelled to give his son more money in proportion to the amount he possessed. Who really has a right to pose such a question other than the man himself? My friend may discuss the situation and believe this man to be ungenerous, but does he know all of the facts? Does he know what his son wants the money for, how hard the son works or indeed how hard his friend may have worked for the money in question? The answer is probably not. Such questions of generosity are not there for 'outsiders' to contemplate.

We need to look at the way we portray ourselves to other people. Accept them for who they are and what they have achieved. I believe God to be a giving God who has planted the tools and provided us with the scoop to nurture them. We ought not begrudge a person their success but strive to make our own. Yes, I believe we are not all at the same advantage as each other but equally that doesn't mean we should give up hope to achieve.

Remember that borrowing or utilising what isn't yours can never last. Jesus Christ taught His disciples such a lesson and prepared them for what they would be required to face by warning them that it was necessary that He should die but assuring them that He would be raised from the dead.

'The wicked borrows but does not pay back, but the righteous is generous and gives' (Psalm 37:21 ESV).

During my day-to-day working life, I always tried to achieve the best I could at what ever I ventured into. Because of this attitude I was labelled a workaholic. It didn't bother me because I know that working hard never did anyone any harm. But it bothered others; they could never understand why I applied myself in that way. Why do we always try to form opinions on the actions of others? For me, however, we should not judge the actions or intentions of others, for you never really know the circumstances that surround their decision.

If we are not able to appreciate another person's generosity, even if it doesn't match our expectation, then we cannot possibly be happy within ourselves. Respecting and acknowledging the generosity of others is a crucial lesson that we need to teach future generations. Remember they are the future, and we are not leading them with a strong example of behaviour, then how can their futures be bright?

'Let no corrupting talk come out of your mouths, but only such as is good for building up, as fits the occasion, that it may give grace to those who hear' (Ephesians 4:29 ESV).

There are some great and fun ways to drive home and teach the lessons of generosity to children—our future. I've listed a sample here as a way for you to reflect on how you can support our future generations with their learning of this crucial life skill. Such exercises can be used by any of us at any time, no matter how old we are, to re-focus our intention on following through on the essential act of never giving to receive.

1. Ask your children to go through the pantry at home and find any canned goods that haven't been used within the last six months. If they're not being eaten, give them to a family who can use them.
2. Direct your children to set aside a certain percentage of their allowance, job money, or money that came through gifts for the purpose of giving to charity. Then help them choose a charity that is meaningful to them, allow them to research it and motivate them to write the letter telling the charity how much and why they want to donate to them.

3. Visit an assisted living facility or a nursing home so that your children can sing songs, play games and read with the seniors there.
4. After every other season, have a 'wardrobe day' in which your children spend some time going through their clothes and bagging up the things that are too small or unused. Then drive them to the drop off centre or charity and allow them to contribute their donations.
5. Ask your children to help make cards or wrap presents for people outside of your family and circle of friends. Perhaps these contributions could be for the local children's hospital or other charity.
6. Invite someone who doesn't have family nearby to share a meal or come over for a movie. You wouldn't believe how grateful they will be just to feel included.
7. Talk to your children often about generosity, giving and how they can give of themselves each day. It's amazing that the more we give, the more we get out of living.
8. Encourage your children to call elderly family members—even extended family members– just to say hello, tell them what's new and ask them what they're up to these days. A simple call can make someone's day.
9. Ensure that your children send out thank you cards. If they're very young, have them sign them in their own way—either with their name, a drawing or decorative stickers.

10. Read books that illustrate the power of giving. Talk about the characters with your children and ask them how each character showed generosity of spirit. What did they admire?
11. Whenever you give your time, talent, thanks or treasures to others, let your children know how good it makes you feel, how it helps others and why you do it. When they see and hear about you doing it, it will be more natural for them to do it as well. It will simply be 'something your family does'.
12. Give within your family as well as outside of your family. When you ask your children 'what kind of family are we?' they should be able to answer with the top five values that define your family. Make generosity one of them.
13. Refrain from giving material rewards for giving generously. It's counter intuitive to reward a child for giving by giving him or her money or more toys. Generosity should be tied to internal gratification not external motivators.
14. Talk about what other people need rather than just what the child wants. Notice the people around you and help your children to do the same. When you visit the local hospital, encourage your children to look around and ask them: 'if you were here, what do you wish you had?' Let's take a look at the books and games they have, what's missing? When we encourage our children to focus on others, we

help them remember that generosity is more important than more gifts for him or herself.

15. Before your child's birthday or birthday party, ask him or her which toys she can contribute to others. If he or she receives 10 new gifts, what are the 10 toys or games from her current stash that she can donate to someone in need?

16. Reward spontaneous generosity by praising it. Let your children know when you see a great example of generosity. Praise the person who showed the generosity in front of your children and privately.

17. After your children have given something—talk about it. How do they feel? Who do they think their old favourite shirt will go to now? How will their old favourite toy feel to be loved by another little boy or girl who will be so happy to have a teddy bear to love? What do they think the lady at the nursing home will say when she opens the card your child made with all the stickers on it?

18. Each day ask what the family is grateful for and how they showed generosity.

As Acts 20:35 ESV says, 'One gives freely, yet grows all the richer; another withholds what he should give, and only suffers want. Whoever brings blessing will be enriched, and one who waters will himself be watered'.

CHAPTER 6
Parental Influence

In Chapter 5 we looked at how we, as parents, relatives, loved ones or friends of children, can help teach children the importance of generosity and of giving to others. In this chapter, I touch on how we can work with our children to teach them to become morally grounded individuals, using the Bible as a basis for this teaching.

I believe that the best book that any Christian can possess and refer to is the Bible; it is particularly helpful in both study and for on-going reference. By using the Bible as a reference, we can pass on its wisdom, and our own, to our children.

Romans 12:2 says, 'Do not be conformed to this world, but be transformed by the renewal of your mind, that by testing you may discern what is the will of God, what is good and acceptable and perfect'.

How do we get to a point where we can train ourselves to act in such a way and indeed pass on what we have learnt to our children? Ultimately, it all begins in the way in which we raise our children.

Moral development in a child is as important as physical or cognitive development, which makes it a crucial part of parenting. Teaching morals can be tricky, especially because children develop gradually in this area. Good moral behaviour includes honesty, kindness, generosity, loyalty, empathy, respect and forgiveness. It is important to understand ways you can help pass on morals and teach right from wrong in any stage of your child's moral development.

Step 1

Talk to your child about what good moral behaviour looks like. Use opportunities, such as storybook plots or movies, to discuss what is right and wrong. Ask him how he would feel in certain situations.

Step 2

Set an example in your daily life. Treat your child with fairness, kindness and empathy and treat other adults and family members that way as well. If you encourage your child's moral development only verbally and do not demonstrate how morals work, he or she may not grasp the concept as well. Dr Robert Coles, a child psychiatrist, says your child measures you by your actions.

Step 3

Respect your child and make it clear that he must respect you in return. Ohio State University Extension states that requiring courtesy and respect can help your child realise that respect should be given to adults and caregivers.

Step 4

Weigh your child's opinions before determining rules or disciplinary actions. Even if you choose not to reflect his or her opinions in your final decision, you are showing that his or her thoughts are valued. This exhibits fairness and contributes to moral understanding by helping him or her realise that every point of view is important.

Step 5

Give your child age-appropriate household chores so he or she can begin to understand the importance of responsibility; encourage your child to volunteer for a service project or donate items to charity. This helps him understand the importance of giving, as outlined in Chapter 5.

Step 6

Spend as much quality time with your child as possible. Ohio State University Extension states that parents who spend quality time with their children and combine that with abundant love have children with higher moral development.[5]

Parenting is the most difficult task you will ever undertake. From a young age, it is necessary to teach a child about respect, self-control, morals and values. 'Train up a child in the way he should go; even when he is old he will not depart from it' (Proverbs 22:6).

It is also important to teach our children that they are each unique, special and that their creation is in itself a wonder to rejoice. God, the creator of all things, took the time to make them in their mother's womb. They have a purpose in life. We must teach them that

---

[5] http://www.livestrong.com

they are precious to God. We must teach them the meaning of repentance, sin and God's holiness from a very young age.

As parents or guardians of children, it is important to monitor and influence how they view the world in order to ensure that they start life in a well-informed and well-balanced manner. Part of this process can come from monitoring what our children watch on the television, encouraging them to watch educational programmes that are appropriate for their age.

Guiding children's television viewing is easier said than done. Television is a pervasive medium throughout society. Here are some interesting facts about young children and television, and guidelines for monitoring its usage.

- A report, 'Zero to Six: Electronic Media in the Lives of Infants, Toddlers, and Pre-schoolers', revealed:
    - 36 per cent of children have a TV in their bedroom.
    - Children with TVs in the bedroom watch an average of twenty-two more minutes of TV than children without them.
    - 43 per cent of parents think that TV helps children learn.
    - 77 per cent of children can operate a TV by themselves.
    - Children with parents who do not make rules about TV viewing watch an

average of 29 more minutes of TV per day than children whose parents have such rules.

How should we, as responsible parents, friends or guardians, influence children's television viewing in a positive way? Here are some ideas:

- Set rules and guidelines early. Just like most habits, habits related to television viewing begin early. Therefore, it's better to develop good habits regarding television viewing early in life rather than have to try and break old habits later in childhood. Some basic rules and limits include:
    o Limit the amount of time children spend watching television. A general public consensus is that most children spend more time than they should in front of the TV. The American Academy of Paediatrics recommends that children's television viewing be limited to no more than one or two hours a day.
    o Avoid watching television during meals. Television viewing during meals sets bad habits relating to family conversations and interactions.
    o Monitor children's television viewing. Children should not be permitted to watch adult television, violent

programs or violent cartoons. This means that parents and other adults who are responsible for children have to screen and monitor what their children watch. When children are allowed to watch violent television, they not only learn violent and aggressive behaviour, they also become desensitised to violence.

- Keep televisions out of children's bedrooms. Generally speaking, children should not be permitted to have a television in their room; however, as our statistics show, 36 per cent of children do have one in their room! When children have a television in their bedroom, their television viewing is not monitored and they can and do watch whatever they want.
- Don't use television as a babysitter. Television is not able to care for, protect or nurture children. In other words, television cannot take the place of a parent. Likewise, television should not be used as a means of 'keeping children busy'.
- Participate with children. Parents should watch television with their children. This way parents can discuss program content with their children and can clarify actions and behaviours.
- Be a good role model. Parents can be good role models when they set good examples by the programs they watch. Parents should not view

television with adult, sexual or violent content when children are present.
- Help children learn from television. The majority of parents believe that children learn from television. So, encourage parents to watch educational shows with their children.[6]

Instead of relying on electronic devices such as televisions to entertain, interact and stimulate children, we should focus on personal contact and involvement with our children, especially if we want to help them establish solid and positive personalities. As mentioned in volume one of my book *From the Bottom to the Top*, we should sit and listen to our child or children and ask questions, such as 'how are you doing?' 'Is there anything going on in school?' 'How are your friends?'

'Education is our passport to the future, for tomorrow belongs to the people who prepare for it today'—Malcolm X.

We therefore have to ensure that this need for education is wider than that found within schools or other academic or learning environments. It is important to teach our children the fundamental values and morals that they need to grow to become positive, caring and 'good' individuals. Whilst this is a huge task, and one that will of course lead to errors and difficulties along the way, committing yourself to teaching children the value of life and the importance

---

[6] www.education.com

of ethical grounding will ultimately pay dividends for them and for society in the future.

CHAPTER 7
We all have Choices

In Chapters 5 and 6, we explored the way in which we can help influence the youth of today; working with children from an early age instils a sense of generosity, morality and positive spirit into the future generation. In this chapter, the emphasis of learning changes slightly to focus on adult interactions and decision making—lessons that can of course be used to influence those around us, including the children for whom we are responsible.

In this chapter, the focus is on how our choices make us who we are. No matter what the situation and no matter how hard it might seem, eventually we will make a decision that will lead us down a path be it right or wrong. It is the determination to seek out and choose the right choice that can identify the morally strong. Of course there is a need to keep some level of perspective – no human being is perfect and we will all at some point choose an option or make a decision that isn't ethically correct or morally right. However those strong individuals amongst us will identify this error in their actions and will continue to strive for the right choices as they continue through the tricky and winding path of life. Romans 8.7 says, 'for the mind that is set on the flesh is hostile to God, for it does not submit to God's law; indeed, it cannot'.

The information and guidance found in the rest of this chapter is based on the thoughts and ideas put forward by Christopher Hansard in his blog, 'The

Choices You Make—How to Make the Right Choices'. As a fellow believer in spirituality and self-knowledge, I agree whole-heartedly with his thoughts and views on supporting individuals to make positive choices that will ultimately define them. As the Bible states, 'the good person out of his good treasure brings forth good, and the evil person out of his evil treasure brings forth evil' (Matthew 12:35).

We are all faced with choices, and choices can tip the balance in our lives from going nowhere to suddenly arriving where you have always wanted to be. At the end of the day, all options or (all choices so to speak) are available to us, except the understanding of what a choice is and what you can do with it. The power of choice is so huge that it often misses our perceptions entirely. Choices define who we become and who we used to be. Choices change our lives.

Many other influential powers tell us that choice is our right; we have the right to choose. Choice is everywhere, so much so, that most people do not know what choice really is as they have so many options available to them on a daily basis. After a while, people switch off and their hearts close down a little, their minds get a little narrower, and they think that choice is what to buy for dinner or what is best for them only.

We may have more material choices than our forefathers did, but as to whether a wide range of choice is any better is yet to be seen. Mankind has always traded, creating a choice of goods, ideas, options for belief and behaviour, yet if I asked you what choices you have in your life today, right now, I wonder what you would say?

Could you give me a list?

Most people would believe that deep within them that they have little freedom of choice, that there are not many choices to be made, and, as far as their life goes, they have to do the best with what they have.

We are told we have choices, but not how to make them. We are encouraged to make choices, but often only within a set framework of our culture, our neighbourhood, our family's opinions, our views of how the world should be. Often, our range of choices is limited because our daily life is beset with the difficulties of daily living or the increasing intolerance and self-destruction of the world around us. Often, we do not know what our choices are made of or where they come from.

Yet, each of us has more choice than we can consciously know; when we make a conscious choice we transform our reality. We get bigger within. When this takes place the world sits up and takes notice, supporting this as the natural evolution of your inner self.

Are you aware of the affect that the choices you have made have had upon your life or upon other people? Are you afraid of making choices, so you let other people make them for you?

There comes a time in your life when you must make a choice and take a risk on living. Making a choice is taking a risk. When you make a choice you give birth to the spiritual, emotional and material energies latent within you.

A choice is an act of creation. If you want to create something good, be prepared to make a choice. The questions you need to ask yourself are:

1. If I do not make choices for myself then how do I start?
2. If you make choices already, then ask yourself the following:
    a. What are my choices fuelled by? Are they just a response to my circumstances or do they come from inner change?
    b. What is behind my choices and are they really good for me?

The ability to make the right choice or any choice at all comes from knowing where you are in your life and where you are within yourself.

To empower your choices ask yourself this question: do you make your life, or does life make you do things? Some people would say that they make their own life, whilst others feel that they should just accept what happens.

The answer is both, to know when to act and to know when not to act. In order to know this, you need to make a fundamental choice: to trust life utterly, thus gaining insight on when to act and when not to, or be pushed around by your reactive mind or circumstances. By making the choice to connect with the life within you, life then reacts positively and supports your choice.

To change your life means changing the choices you make. Here is a list of suggestions that you can try to implement to change your life for the better:

1. Change what you eat and wear daily and to get up one hour earlier than you normally do. In that time, spend some of it on your own, even if its five minutes.
2. Examine your motives behind the way you communicate with others daily.
3. Speak and behave with as much openness and compassion as you can regardless of your mood.
4. Listen with your heart instead of your head to everything you see, read, hear and are told.
5. Change the way you think about, behave towards and judge other people.
6. Appreciate that your life as it currently is, is what you need to have. As part of this, examine if your current work really reflects who you are and can be.
7. Remember that you can take responsibility for your thoughts, actions and speech and be ready to carry this responsibility with care and discipline. As part of this, forgive all the real and imaginary wrongs done to you by other people and ask forgiveness of others that you have wronged. As stated in

the Bible, 'Let all bitterness and wrath and anger and clamour and slander be put away from you, along with all malice. Be kind to one another, tender-hearted, forgiving one another, as God in Christ forgave you' (Ephesians 4:31-32, ESV).
8. Try to trust all that you do and everyone you meet.
9. Regard your daily life as a lesson in humility and peace. Look to be taught lessons by anyone at any time. Remember there is no such thing as a stranger. A stranger is a friend you have yet to know.
10. Remember each day that you are good inside and a worthy of respect as all other people. Do not confuse the person inside with their actions and behaviour.

Then once you do become aware, you can start to make choices that will create a new life and a new way of being.

Choices connect people and make history, your history and the history of your friends, family, neighbourhood, and country. The choices our leaders make affect our daily lives—all of us are connected by the energy of choice.

If just one of us decides to make the choice of becoming who we truly can be, our divine innermost self, that alone would change the negativity in our world. Can you imagine if we all made that conscious choice? The world would change completely from what we understand it to be.

Your life will rise and fall, good and bad will decorate your days, each a testament to your experience, and, as you live more deeply, each choice you make changes from the recognition of an opportunity to the profound recognition of your being and of the love and compassion that heals everything. You will discover that the smallest choice is a window, a path and a sanctuary of the eternal light that blazes in every human being[7].

---

[7] www.blog.christopherhansard.com

CHAPTER 8
Relationships

In Chapters 1, 2 and 3, we explored the way in which adult relationships can be hurtful and emotionally abusive—focusing specifically on the role that jealousy can play in family relationships, the way that individuals can be hungry for power and use this power in a negative way, and the fact that we often choose to ignore the valued opinions of others in order to pursue our own, selfish causes. In this chapter, I want to pick up on this theme once more, looking at why some relationships with family members, friends or loved ones can become toxic. Indeed, many relationships can begin toxic—it's just that initially only one member of that relationship is aware of the negativity.

Aside from a few exceptions, human beings want to be emotionally and physically close to one another—to share a bond. Life is for sharing, and we all seek at least one individual with whom we can share parts of our lives. Yet, conversely, the building of relationships is a task that is challenging and fraught with difficulties. Solid relationships require significant effort, and this can be a challenge. But what is also difficult is the identification of pure or honest relationships and the ability to dismiss or move away from toxic relationships when they become apparent.

Let's look at a fictional example—the story of Sam and Joy. Sam and Joy began their friendship in their

20s when they started working in the same organisation. Sam initially joined the organisation to support the growth in workload. As the business grew, Joy was employed and the two colleagues started to create a friendship.

'Oil and perfume make the heart glad, and the sweetness of a friend comes from his earnest counsel' (Proverbs 27:9ESV).

As the friendship between Sam and Joy developed, they started to leave work at the same time and often went for a drink together to relax after a busy day in the office. Joy wanted the relationship to develop into a strong friendship, but it didn't take long for her to realise that Sam only seemed interested in collecting information that might in some way benefit him. She also started to notice that Sam was continually putting her down, criticising her and belittling her thoughts, opinions and actions. It didn't take long for Joy to realise that Sam told many lies and really couldn't be trusted.

'You destroy those who speak lies; the Lord abhors the bloodthirsty and deceitful man' (Psalm 5:6 ESV).

Joy knew that she needed to end the 'relationship' or 'friendship' with Sam, but she was nervous to do so. She decided to leave the organisation to better her career prospects and leave the difficult relationship with Sam behind. Such action took courage and the ability to identify a toxic relationship.

Toxic relationships are relationships that mutate into something that has the potential, if not corrected, to be extremely harmful to our well-being. These relationships are not necessarily hopeless, but they require substantial and difficult work if they are to be changed into something healthy. The paradox is that in order to have a reasonable chance of turning a toxic relationship into a healthy relationship, we have to be prepared to leave it.

What is a toxic relationship?
According to Thomas Cory, a toxic relationship is a relationship characterised by behaviours on the part of the toxic partner that are emotionally and, not infrequently, physically damaging to their partner. While a healthy relationship contributes to our self-esteem and emotional energy, a toxic relationship damages self-esteem and drains energy. A healthy relationship involves mutual caring, respect and compassion, an interest in our partner's welfare and growth and an ability to share control and decision-making, in short, a shared desire for each other's happiness. A healthy relationship is a safe relationship, a relationship where we can be ourselves without fear, a place where we feel comfortable and secure. A toxic relationship, on the other hand, is not a safe place. A toxic relationship is characterised by insecurity, self-centeredness, dominance and control. We risk our very being by staying in such a relationship. To say a toxic relationship is dysfunctional is, at best, an understatement[8].

---

[8] www.healthscopemag.com

Types of toxic relationships
Even a good relationship may have brief periods of behaviours we could label toxic on the part of one or both partners. Human beings, after all, are not perfect. Few of us have had any formal education in how to relate to others. We often have to learn as we go, hoping that our basic style of relating to significant others—often learned from our parents and/or friends—is at least reasonably effective.

However, in a toxic relationship, dysfunction rules. The toxic partner engages in inappropriate controlling and manipulative behaviours pretty much on a daily basis.

A toxic individual behaves the way he or she does essentially for one reason: he or she must be in complete control and must have all the power in his or her relationship. Power sharing does not occur in any significant way in a toxic relationship, and, while power struggles are normal in any relationship, particularly in the early stages of a marriage, toxic relationships are characterised by one partner absolutely insisting on being in control.

Let's look at the types of toxic relationships you could come across:

Deprecator-belittler
As in the story of Sam and Joy, this type of toxic individual will constantly belittle you. He or she will make fun of you, essentially implying that pretty much anything you say that expresses your ideas, beliefs or wants is silly or stupid.

The 'bad temper' toxic partner

Often these individuals have an unpredictable and 'hair-trigger' temper. Their partners or friends often describe themselves as 'walking on egg shells' around the toxic partner, never quite knowing what will send him or her into a rage. This constant need for vigilance and inability to know what will trigger an angry outburst wears on both the receiver's emotional and physical health.

The guilt-inducer

The guilt inducer controls by encouraging you to feel guilty any time you do something he or she doesn't like. Not infrequently, they will get someone else to convey their sense of 'disappointment' or 'hurt' to you. For example, your father calls up to tell you how disappointed your mother was that you didn't come over for Sunday dinner.

The overreactor/deflector

If you've ever tried to tell a significant other that you're unhappy, hurt, or angry about something they did, and you somehow find yourself taking care of **their** unhappiness, hurt or anger, you're dealing with an overreactor/deflector. You find yourself comforting them instead of getting comfort. Even worse, you feel bad about yourself for being 'so selfish' that you brought up something that upset your partner so much. Needless to say, your initial concern, hurt or irritation gets lost as you remorsefully take care of your partner's feelings.

The 'independent' (non-dependable) toxic controller
This individual frequently disguises his or her toxic controlling behaviour as simply asserting his or her 'independence'. I'm not going to let anyone control me', is their motto. This toxic individual will rarely keep his or her commitments. Actually, what these individuals are up to is controlling you by keeping you uncertain about what they're going to do.

The user
Users—especially at the beginning of a relationship—often seem to be very nice, courteous and pleasant individuals. And they are, as long as they're getting everything they want from you. A relationship with a user toxic has a one-way nature; you will end up never having done enough for them. There are aspects of this type of relationship in the relationship between Sam and Joy.[9]

Why do people behave in toxic ways, and why do others put up with such behaviour?
The answer is often the same for both individuals: poor self-esteem rooted in underlying insecurity. Toxic individuals behave the way they do because, at some level, they don't believe they are lovable and/or that anyone would really willingly want to meet their needs. Their partners or friends stay with toxic individuals because they too believe they are unlovable and that no one would willingly meet their needs.

---

[9] www.healthscopemag.com

What to do

Ultimately, you can't change the individual who has adopted a toxic standpoint. Joy could not change Sam's behaviour even if she really wanted to. However, we can all change our own attitudes and actions, which may either break us free from such toxic relationships or change the dynamics of the relationship in such a way that the toxic individual makes a conscious decision to also change for the better.

1 Corinthian 10:13ESV reads, 'No temptation has overtaken you that is not common to man. God is faithful, and he will not let you be tempted beyond your ability, but with the temptation he will also provide the way of escape, that you may be able to endure it'.

CHAPTER 9
Love Conquers All

Looking at toxic relationships was the focal point of Chapter 8. Here, in Chapter 9, we are going to explore how love and loving relationships can triumph and blossom when encouraged and how with patience, understanding and commitment, we as individuals can ensure that love does conquer all even if at times it feels as if such victory is impossible to reach.

Many, renowned authors, poets, artists and song writers have picked up on the theme of 'love triumphs', for such a theme is embedded within society, and it is, in many ways, crucial to our own optimism, motivation and way of life. There are a number of quotations that bring out the core concepts that underpin the ideal that love can overcome anything, and, to provide some food for thought before we delve into the heart of this chapter, I have provided a selection of such quotations here:

'I believe that imagination is stronger than knowledge. That myth is more potent than history. That dreams are more powerful than facts. That hope always triumphs over experience. That laughter is the only cure for grief. And I believe that love is stronger than death'.[10]

---

[10] Robert Fulghum

'Perseverance, secret of all triumphs.[11]

To explore the theme that love conquers all and to discuss the fact that sometimes loving relationships experience problems that need faith and love to help resolve, I am going to use the story of Angela and Anthony—a young couple that needed to trust in their love for one another to enable their marriage to survive.

Anthony was adopted by his two parents, Stephen and Mary, when he was a tiny baby. Both successful career-driven individuals, Anthony grew up in a wealthy household where he learnt the importance of self-motivation, hard work and financial security. He enjoyed learning and studying, and when the time came for him to choose his professional path in life; he opted for law and trained to become a barrister.

When Anthony was a teenager, his mother started to become unwell. She found her body wasn't as quick as it had been previously, her muscles stiffened and made her movements slow and cumbersome, and she began shaking constantly. The doctor diagnosed Mary with Parkinson's disease and Mary sadly had to give up her job as a successful lawyer. As time passed and Mary's condition deteriorated, it became obvious that Stephen needed to hire a carer to support in her day-to-day management. And so Angela was hired, a young carer who had a fantastic spirit and personality, someone who cared lovingly for Mary and who blended beautifully with the family unit.

---

[11] Victor Hugo

It didn't take long for Anthony and Angela to fall in love. Unfortunately, as their love blossomed, the Mary's health deteriorated. Stephen too began to fall victim to ill health. Medically retired after an accident at work, he became more and more reliant on Angela for his day-to-day needs. A marriage in the family certainly helped raise spirits, as Anthony and Angela eventually wed in the local church. Their happiness was interrupted by the death of Mary and, shortly afterwards, the unexpected death of Stephen who appeared to give up on life as soon as his wife left his side.

Whilst grief hung over Anthony and Angela for months following the death of Anthony's parents, a sense of normality resumed. Anthony became busier and busier at work and spent less and less time at home. Angela dedicated her time to community life and to the church, yet she felt her life was far from complete, as her husband spent less and less time with her. She tried to understand his work commitments but soon found that she resented the independent life he had carved out without her. Anger, frustration and bitterness took hold, and she eventually booked an appointment for the two of them to meet with the local priest to discuss this difficulty that plagued their marriage.

Anthony loved Angela and did not want to lose her. He willingly met with the priest and explained openly that he loved Angela more than anything; he recognised that she felt neglected and he wanted to address his work/life balance, but this wasn't always achievable when the pressures at work rendered it impossible for him to reduce his workload.

Angela listened but dismissed his comments. She tearfully explained that she felt that Anthony loved his work more than he loved her, and she declared that she couldn't continue to live in this way. She wanted a divorce, and she wanted half of their possessions: a car, half of the house value and half of the money in their bank account. Anthony was shocked and saddened.

The priest asked Angela if she was sure of this decision. He quoted Ephesians 4:26-27ESV: 'Be angry and do not sin; do not let the sun go down on your anger, and give no opportunity to the devil'.

He then turned to Anthony and asked what he wanted and how he felt. Anthony's response was simple. He wanted his wife. He wanted Angela, and he would do all he could to ensure she always felt the same way.

The priest asked them both if they loved each other, and they both confirmed that they did. He smiled and said that love is all they need and that with love they will find a way to overcome these difficulties and find a balance and way of life that made them both happy.

And they did.

Every marriage experiences problems. No matter how long you have been married—whether one year or 40 years—you will have problems. Marital problems can be extremely intense and painful, and those hurts can cut deeply and last a very long time.

The pain caused by someone you care about as much as your spouse may be very difficult to deal with.

Most of us have preconceived ideas about how our spouses should treat us. We expect mistreatment from other people but not from our spouses. Just remember that as human beings, we often think, feel and behave in ways that are hurtful even toward those we love. Flawed people treat each other in flawed ways, so no matter how much we care; we'll sometimes hurt each other.

Your marriage isn't doomed because you hurt one another, have difficulty communicating or have disagreements over important issues. Couples have been experiencing and solving problems on their own, beginning with Adam and Eve, and continue to do so to this day. The more experience and maturity a couple develops in a marriage, the more success is gained in managing and solving problems. God created us with the ability to successfully manage relationships in a healthy and productive way[12]. Remember, 'For nothing will be impossible with God' (Luke 1:37ESV).

Love is the greatest gift we can give and that we can receive. It is important to hold onto it and cherish it and to *believe* in it even when times are hard. 1 Corinthians 13 celebrates the importance of love:

> Though I speak with the tongues of men and of angels, but have not love, I have become sounding brass or a clanging cymbal.

---

[12] Focusonthefamily.com

And though I have the gift of prophecy, and understand all mysteries and all knowledge, and though I have all faith, so that I could remove mountains, but have not love, I am nothing.

And though I bestow all my goods to feed the poor, and though I give my body to be burned, but have not love, it profits me nothing.

Love suffers long and is kind; love does not envy; love does not parade itself, is not puffed up;

Does not behave rudely, does not seek its own, is not provoked, and thinks no evil;

Does not rejoice in iniquity, but rejoices in the truth;

Bears all things, believes all things, hopes all things, endures all things.

Love never fails. But whether there are prophecies, they will fail; whether there are tongues, they will cease; whether there is knowledge, it will vanish away.

For we know in part and we prophesy in part.

But when that which is perfect has come, then that which is in part will be done away?

When I was a child, I spoke as a child, I understood as a child, I thought as a child; but when I became a man, I put away childish things.

For now we see in a mirror, dimly, but then face to face. Now I know in part, but then I shall know just as I also am known.

And now abide faith, hope, love, these three; **but the greatest of these** is **love.**

CHAPTER 10
God heal my pain

One of the most important discoveries concerns an attitude that is present before communication can begin in a time of pain. The attitude is called 'acceptance' yet most of us do not accept. Most of us assume that in order to develop our character, we must tell the other person what we do not like about them. We load our speech with preaching, admonishing and commanding—all of which convey non-recognition of another person's pain. In many families, verbal communication consists only of criticism.

In this inspiring story, a woman called Anna communicates her feelings and attitudes of acceptance in a number of ways to a man named Fred. Many times the lines of communication between them both are severed because the man detects feelings of rejection. Consequently, the man will refrain from expressing his true feelings and thoughts to spare himself pain. It isn't enough for both of them to feel acceptance. Fred must be able to convey these feelings of acceptance in terms that Anna can readily understand.

This was not mandatory for both of them, but it was a voluntary act of showing feelings, motivated by Christian love by Christians who were gifted, but have no children. Not everyone is called to this magnitude of showing feelings in time of pain, not all Christian people have the grace to sell good things when going through pain and sorrow. This took them back to (1 Samuel 1:5, 10KJV), 'but unto Hannah he gave a worthy portion; for he loved Hannah: but the LORD had shut up her womb. And she was in bitterness of soul, and prayed unto the LORD, and wept sore'.

One of the easiest methods of conveying this kind of acceptance by both of them is the saying, 'I understand what you mean' or 'I see what you're saying'. To offer assistance and guidance if needed in their activities would show that you trust in their ability. However, if both were corrected and given advice on their mistakes, Anna may not have become resentful or discouraged. 'I can never do anything to please my husband. What's the use?' Fred may not have meant to send a message of rejection, but he did. Just like in 1 Samuel 1:13-14KJV, 'Now Hannah, she spoke in her heart; only her lips moved, but her voice was not heard: therefore Eli thought she had been drunken. And Eli said unto her, How long wilt thou be drunken? Put away thy wine from thee'.

Hannah replied (1 Samuel 1:15-16KJV), 'And Hannah answered and said, no my lord, I am a woman of a sorrowful spirit: I have drunk neither wine nor strong drink, but have poured out my soul before the LORD. Count not thine handmaid for a daughter of Belial: for out of the abundance of my complaint and grief have I spoken hitherto'.

Very often when we are married, we move in, join in or check up on each other to see if we are really helping each other measure up to our expectations. Although both Anne and Fred married young they did not bear any children. This affected their self-worth either positively or negatively. Such realisation had closed them both up, but passive listening allowed them to open up, talk about the situation and move toward solving the problem on their own. Her mother's passive listening along with her accompanying body language conveyed her interest and acceptance of her child's feelings.

Few people have mastered this skill. They seem to feel it their duty to correct, refute, admonish, restate or reinterpret everything people said to them both. Fred and Anna live together above their busy high street convenience shop. How hard both of them found it to express their feelings in an atmosphere of acceptance in which they could have more easily had moved toward solving their problems of pain. Their most read book (Galatians 6:9-10) says, 'and let us not be weary in well doing: for in due season we shall reap it we faint not. As we have the opportunity, let us do well unto all men, especially unto them who are of the household of faith'.

However, no one can remain silent long in a good relationship. *Did* they have the opportunity to create circumstances when the time might be appropriate to communicate? They both believed that opportunity abounded everywhere, but the needs around them were enormous; there were needs everywhere to be met. They looked for these opportunities and made themselves available to meet needs and alleviate human suffering.

The kind of response Fred and Anna got determined if they would continue to open up to others. An effective verbal response for both of them was the 'tell-me-more' invitation. This kind of communication is a door opener that does not communicate a judgmental evaluation of what each is trying to say. Both replied, 'how interesting', 'I'm happy to hear that', 'Good!' 'Great!' 'I see', 'I understand'.

More explicit 'tell-me-mores' for both of them are 'I can see how important this is to you', 'tell me more about this', 'I'd be interested in hearing what you have to say about this' or 'I'd like to hear your point of view'. Such responses reveal mutual interest and that each has the right to express his or her feelings. It reveals that they might learn something from each other, that they'd like to hear each other's point of view and that their ideas are equally important. They both try to keep up the conversation with each other.

Fred and Anna's moving in together had made them a lot closer yet Anna could not help but feel angry. Fred was very sick he had cancer and it was terminal. Anna held Fred in her arms looked down at him and prayed the Lord would take away his suffering and restore him back to her in good health. However this was not to be Fred slowly slipped away and died in her arms in the bedroom.

Anna thinks that it is not possible to totally communicate everything about her husband passing away and the pain and sorrow that first came to her. She read the words of Solomon from (Proverbs 28:27), 'He that giveth unto the poor shall not lack: but he that hideth of his eyes shall have many a curse'. Thinking about all the wonderful memories she had made with her husband, Anna wonder how she was going to cope without Fred, it was inconceivable. She was consumed by pain and sorrow by the loss of Fred, and began to weep uncontrollably.

Anna opened the door of the house sobbing, 'I wish I didn't have such a loving husband! She's was in great pain, and the sorrow of the passing away of her husband Fred weighed heavy on her. You might have thought, 'Anna! What a dreadful thing to say!' because you know she really loved him. But by saying that, you are denying Anna feelings of pain and sorrow. Often, when others share emotions with us, we proceed to tell them how they should or should not feel—as though our statements of logic can erase their pain and sorrowful feelings! We do this because we have been taught that negative feelings are bad and that we shouldn't have them.

As a result, Anna felt less worthy or even worthless when such feelings arose in her. Yet, negative feelings are a fact of life. She couldn't live from day to day without conflicts, yet conflicts engender negative emotions. Tragically, after two years of marriage, Anna was left alone by herself. Anna coped with her emotions of pain and sorrow by finding other ways to accept her feelings, by providing acceptable outlets, such as engaging in active hobbies and even old-fashioned charitable organisation work.

Looking at the Apostles (James 1:17), 'Every good gift and every perfect gift is from above, and cometh down from the father of lights, with whom is no variableness, neither shadow of turning'. God is the Giver of our resources; we owe everything we have to Him, without Him we cannot have what we have. He has the ability to give whatever we need or ask for, as long as it is consistent with His will. (Matthew 7:11), 'If ye then, being evil, know how to give good gifts unto your children, how much more shall your Father which is in heaven give good gifts to them that ask him'.

If you have not identified Anna's feelings properly, you will not likely know what she meant or even understand her. At times, it will be necessary for us to prod gently to uncover the feelings behind the words of someone who has suffered pain and sorrow. Anyone like Anna in the grip of emotional pain and sorrow cannot think clearly; by assisting her to express plain and sorrow aloud, you are helping her to learn how to handle the negative feelings of her husband's death in a positive way.

This classic example revolves around Anna. She always busied herself helping people and working with charitable organisations. She often wondered why her life was so ugly. What she really meant was why had life been so mean to her? Why couldn't her life be a pretty picture, painted on a glowing background? Anna could find no answers. To Anna, her life was routine; all she did was cook for the homeless and those less fortunate around her.

The secret of Anna offering her faith was written in Hebrew 11:4, 'By faith Abel offered unto God a more excellent sacrifice than Cain, by which he obtained a witness that he was righteous, God testifying of his gifts; and by it be being dead yet speaketh'. Anna's faith does not worry about the cost of her giving because the giver trusts God enough to meet her personal needs and that her life is divinely 'insured' and 'assured' against lack or poverty.

Yes, Anna really felt something special when she was with those homeless people. She made it her business to always be very prayerful and she believed that the Almighty God would not give her anything bigger than what she could handle. It was a really good, fulfilling job. Anna believed that doing good and pleasing everyone was the best policy in life.

She believed that God clearly told the Israelites to help the poor among them when they arrived in the Promised Land. This was an important condition for their possessing their land. The poor must not be ignored and those who were blessed must not close their eyes and hands toward them. So pain or no pain, she knew what her husband would do.

God spoke through Moses to His people (Deut.15:7), 'If there be among you a poor man of one of thy brethren within any of thy gates in thy land which the LORD thy God given thee, thou shalt not harden thine heart, nor shut thine hand from thy poor brother'. When Anna considered the poor, she believed God would consider her pain and sorrow and deliver her from her own troublesome pains. Local community people come to her for advice and help, which she freely gave. She believes that one day God will hear her prayers.

One morning, whilst Anna was praying, she heard a voice say, 'I am God, do not worry'. As the Bible says in (Matthew 7:7): 'Ask and it will be given to you;

seek, and you will find; knock and it will be opened to you'. It bothered her to leave the conversation unfinished because she felt that little or nothing had been resolved. But as she reviewed the comments in her mind, she realised that God had begun to move into the solving the problem of her pain and sorrow. Could this mean that the many questions she had that bothered her would finally be answered?

Later that same morning, the voice said to Anna, 'I will visit and eat with you today quiet firmly with confidents'. She reasoned to herself that she wasn't hearing right. But the voice said again: 'I will visit and eat with you today!' This made Anne happy. What does all this mean, she wondered? Is God coming to visit me, to eat with me?

He is the One who sees our secret giving and rewards us openly or publicly. She began to read (Matthew 10:41-42), 'He that receiveth a prophet in the name of a prophet shall receive a prophet's reward; and he that receiveth a righteous man in the name of a righteous man shall receive a righteous man's reward. And whosoever shall give to drink unto one of these little ones a cup of cold water only in the name of a disciple, verily I say unto you, he shall in no wise lose his reward'.

Anna woke up early that morning and started cooking. After that, she opened her door as normal, trying to listen and look for this God that was coming to eat with her. Many people passed by and she continued assisting them in the same way as always, while her anger, frustration and other feelings went untouched. Hostility and recriminations were rampant.

She needed someone to take a firm stand with her. In the mid-morning, a beggar passing by her home asked for something to eat, so Anna gave food to the beggar freely.

The beggar said, 'For promotion cometh neither from the east, nor from the west, nor from the south. But God is the judge: he putteth down one, and setteth up another' (Psalm 75:6-7). Anne sat observed that everyone who passed in front of her home that day needed something to eat; she gave as she anxiously waited for God. Anne had so much she wanted to say. There were ample opportunities for each person that passed to listen to her words and, more importantly, the emotions behind them. It finally came to light that Anna had found that her food was for people in great need and the more she gave the more she found that nothing was wasted.

Two days later, a man came by looking very hungry and asked Anna for food, but Anna told the man the food she had left was just enough for God. Feeling sorry for the man, Anna told him she would give him the food and cook some more food for God. The man replied, 'The blessing of God maketh rich and addeth no sorrows with it' (Prov. 10:22). So Anne started to prepare more food and continued waiting for God. Finally, the doorbell rang and a voice said, 'I need to speak to you'. So she went to the front door, feeling good to have everything ready for God in time. But when she opened the door, she found no one.

As it grew late, she felt disappointed that God did not show up as He had promised her. It wasn't long afterwards that Anna heard the voice again saying, 'Anne, you are a kind woman. I shall supply all your needs. Your, meals have not wasted. I have blessed your diligence and hard work'.

The voice startled Anna at first, and then she answered, 'God, are you still coming to visit me'? God replied, 'Anna, I have visited you, I have walked with you, I have eaten with you, and I have sat with you. I am with you always Anna. Communication is a two-way street. The timing is important. If listening doesn't settle the matter, then talk. It was evident that I was pleased with your work and that your service on earth was not yet finished. I am God, I am the God that is omnipresent, whose presence fills everywhere, yet I do come and go. So, Anna, I have visited you. This is because though His presence is everywhere; His manifested presence is not everywhere.

As stated in 1 John 3:1: 'See what kind of love the Father has given to us that we should be called children of God; and so we are. The reason why the world does not know us is that it did not know him'. This was, indeed, a miracle. Her generosity and hospitality had healed her pain and suffering. So she said: 'God's visit healed my pain'.

Summarises

This book has touched on a number of different subjects that all have one key theme in common—morality. The way, in which we relate to others, the way in which we treat others and indeed the way in which we view our lives and our own actions have all been discussed here. They in turn deepen our understanding of the theme of morality, acceptable social behaviour and ethics.

In Chapter 1, we looked at how family members can turn against you and how their jealousy towards your life and lifestyle can have detrimental effects on your own life. We discussed how to overcome such negativity and suggested the importance of keeping yourself grounded and focused on your own dreams, as opposed to falling into a battle with those who surround you.

In Chapter 2, we reviewed the way in which other individuals can abuse, hurt and belittle you, with a particular focus on friendships. Examples of how friendships have broken down through jealousy were provided, alongside ideas on how to recognise 'false friendships'.

In Chapter 3, the theme of power was discussed and we looked at the different types of power that exist, how power can be used negatively and, importantly, how this can be turned around so that power can be used in a positive and inspiring way.

In Chapter 4, the idea of faith was explored, with a particular focus on God and his omnipotent presence. The need to trust in God and to put your faith in God's almighty's power is reiterated here.

In Chapter 5, the concept of generosity was discussed, and here we not only looked at ways in which we, as adults, can share generously and display generosity, but also ways in which we can encourage our children to do the same.

In Chapter 6, the idea that we can support children to become grounded, kind and strong individuals is put forward. The Bible is there to help us teach children how to have a sense of morality and to display this within their day-to-day lives.

In Chapter 7, the theme was that of choices, as we explored how choices and strategies for making positive and 'right' choices are made.

In Chapter 8, the topic of relationships was re-visited, picking up once more on the notions explored in Chapters 1 and 2 that relationships with those individuals who are closest to you can actually be toxic and detrimental to your own personal happiness. How to recognise a relationship as 'toxic' and how to manage toxic relationships were explored.

In Chapter 9, the focus remained on relationships, but this time we shifted the focus to remind ourselves that true relationships that are built on love can withstand trauma and breakdown, as long as you find the time to reinvest in them, and as long as you believe that, with God's help, together you can overcome setbacks.

In Chapter 10 told a story of healing and faith in God; no matter our condition, we should be patient, and God will heal our pain.

The key message throughout this book is that there are individuals out there who do not hold the same morals as you and will look to hurt you, betray you and defy you. These individuals are often those who know you best and who are closest to you. As frustrating and disappointing as this may seem, remember too that there are so many people out there who love and cherish us— these are the relationships that need our attention, our commitment and our love. It can be difficult identifying true, positive relationships when faced with the prospect that some could be negative. Hopefully, this book has helped you find a way to identify those positive relationships that require your focus. Hopefully, it has also provided some food for thought when it comes to establishing and building positive relationships—relationships that are built on faith, honesty and generosity— for when it comes to teaching children the complex principles of building solid and caring relationships themselves.

www.ingramcontent.com/pod-product-compliance
Lightning Source LLC
LaVergne TN
LVHW041548070426
835507LV00011B/990